CONTENTS

KU-798-275

Words that appear in **bold**
can be found in the glossary
on page 28.

WHO WERE THE ANGLO-SAXONS?

Around the year 400, tribes of warriors began invading Britain, searching for new land where they could settle. The tribes were Angles, Saxons and Jutes, who came from Germany and Denmark, and they were later known as the 'Anglo-Saxons'. After the Anglo-Saxons took over southern Britain, the country gained the name 'Angle-land', or 'England'.

ANGLO-SAXON ENGLAND

Before the Anglo-Saxons arrived, Britain had been part of the Roman Empire, but in 413 the last Roman soldiers left Britain. Once the Romans had left, the Celtic British tribes fought amongst themselves, and their lands became an easy target for invaders.

By 600, thousands of Anglo-Saxon families had settled in southern Britain. Anglo-Saxon England was divided into seven kingdoms, ruled by powerful warrior kings (see map). Meanwhile, the Celts of Britain had mainly retreated into Scotland and Wales.

▶ This map of Anglo-Saxon England shows the seven kingdoms established around the year 800, and also shows the border of the Danish lands created in 887.

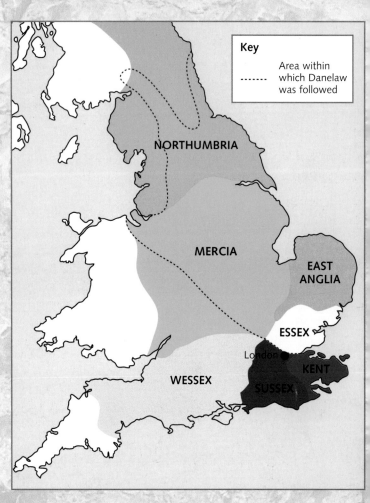

Key

- - - - - Area within which Danelaw was followed

NORTHUMBRIA

MERCIA

EAST ANGLIA

ESSEX

London

KENT

WESSEX

SUSSEX

ANGLO-SAXON TIMELINE

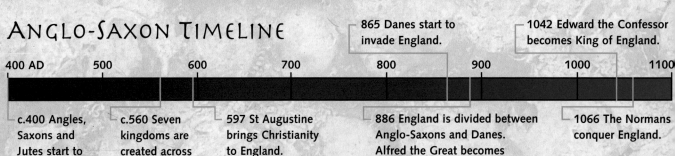

| 400 AD | 500 | 600 | 700 | 800 | 900 | 1000 | 1100 |

865 Danes start to invade England.

1042 Edward the Confessor becomes King of England.

c.400 Angles, Saxons and Jutes start to settle in Britain.

c.560 Seven kingdoms are created across Britain.

597 St Augustine brings Christianity to England.

886 England is divided between Anglo-Saxons and Danes. Alfred the Great becomes King of Western England.

1066 The Normans conquer England.

Anglo-Saxons and Danes

Around 865, new invaders arrived on the east coast of England. They were the Danes – Viking tribes from Denmark. The Danes moved rapidly through eastern England, but they were driven back by King Alfred of Wessex.

Alfred and the Danes agreed to divide England between them. The Danes ruled the north and east while Alfred ruled the south and west. For the next 70 years, some of the rulers of England were Danish kings. Finally, in 1042, the Anglo-Saxon Edward the Confessor became king of all England.

The Norman Conquest

When Edward the Confessor died in 1066, Harold, **Earl** of Wessex became the new English king. But in less than a year, William, Duke of Normandy, led an invasion from France. The Anglo-Saxon period came to an end when William defeated Harold at the Battle of Hastings. William became the first Norman king of England.

▼ The Bayeux Tapestry was completed around 1077 and illustrates the Norman Conquest of England. Here, three Norman knights are shown attacking Anglo-Saxon foot-soldiers.

ANGLO-SAXON MEN, WOMEN AND CHILDREN

Anglo-Saxon society was divided into four main groups, or classes. The most powerful class were the kings and their families. Next came the nobles, known as **thanes**. The largest group were the free people, or **churls**, and there were also slaves, who had no freedom. Thanes, churls and slaves all lived together in small villages. By the end of the Anglo-Saxon period, some villages had grown into towns.

◀ This scene shows a feast in a thane's hall. The thane's slaves did the cooking, kept the fire burning and served everyone with food and drink.

THANES, CHURLS AND SLAVES

The thane and his family lived in a large hall in the heart of the village. He owned the fields and woods around the village as well as herds of cows, pigs and sheep. The churls worked on the thane's land and looked after his animals. Each village family also had their own narrow strips of land in the thane's fields.

Male churls swore **loyalty** to their thane, and promised to fight for him in times of war. In return, the thane promised to do his best to keep all the villagers safe from attack. If the village was attacked, everybody sheltered in the thane's hall.

Slaves were owned by their master and mistress. Most slaves were prisoners of war, who had been captured by the Anglo-Saxons in their battles with the Celts.

HUSBANDS, WIVES AND CHILDREN

In Anglo-Saxon times, men were in charge of their family, but women had rights too. A woman had the right to refuse a marriage that her parents had chosen for her. She could also own land and goods.

Children helped their parents in their farming work and in the home. Girls learned to weave and cook. Boys practised hunting and fishing and trained for battle.

▲ West Stow in Suffolk is a living museum of Anglo-Saxon life. Men, women and children play the parts of Anglo-Saxon farmers and their families.

REAL LIVES

EANSWIDA: A GIRL WHO REFUSED TO MARRY

Eanswida lived in the 7th century and was the daughter of King Eadbald of Kent. She became a Christian when she was very young and loved to spend her time praying. As a teenager, she refused to marry the pagan prince her father had chosen as her husband. Instead she persuaded King Eadbert to help her set up a **convent** at Folkestone in Kent. Eanswida was **abbess** at Folkestone for the rest of her life and also ran the convent farm.

WHO WAS IN CHARGE IN ANGLO-SAXON TIMES?

During the Anglo-Saxon period, England had several different kinds of rulers. From 556, there were seven independent kings, each ruling their own kingdom. Then the Danes invaded and, in 886, England was divided into two large kingdoms, with an Anglo-Saxon and a Danish king. After 924, England had a single Anglo-Saxon ruler, but in 1013 the Danes invaded again and Danish kings took over. England was ruled by the King of Denmark for 30 years before an Anglo-Saxon king gained control in 1042.

WELL-KNOWN KINGS

Famous kings from the Anglo-Saxon period are Canute, Alfred the Great and Edward the Confessor. Canute ruled England from 1016 to 1035. He was a strong ruler who reorganized the country's government. Edward the Confessor was king from 1042 to 1066. He was a very religious man, but a weak ruler. Within a year of his death, England was conquered by Normans.

POWERFUL QUEENS

Some of the early Anglo-Saxon kings had very strong-minded wives, who helped their

◀ A portrait of King Edward the Confessor, painted about 400 years after his death.

husbands to govern their kingdoms. Queen Bertha was the wife of King Ethelbert of Kent. She was one of the first Anglo-Saxons to give up her **pagan** beliefs and become a Christian. Bertha persuaded her husband to **convert** to Christianity, and together they turned Kent into a Christian kingdom.

ADVISORS AND SHERIFFS

Around the year 600, the Anglo-Saxon kings began to hold meetings with the **Witan**, a group of powerful nobles. The members of the Witan advised each king on his country's laws.

In 1017, the Danish King Canute introduced a new way of governing England. He divided the country into four **earldoms**: Northumbria, East Anglia, Mercia and Wessex. Each earldom was run by an earl, and there were also smaller units called 'shires'. The shires were governed by 'shire reeves', who soon became known as 'sheriffs'.

REAL LIVES

ALFRED THE GREAT

King Alfred of Wessex led the Anglo-Saxons in their fight against the Danes. He drove the Danes out of Wessex, Sussex, Kent and Mercia, and all these kingdoms became part of Alfred's land. From 874 to his death in 899, Alfred ruled western England. He defended his kingdom against invaders, building walled towns close to the coast, and setting up a navy. He also encouraged art and learning in his kingdom.

WHAT WAS FAMILY LIFE LIKE IN ANGLO-SAXON TIMES?

Family life was very important in Anglo-Saxon times. All the families in a village had strong loyalties to each other and to their thane. For most Anglo-Saxon people, the only way to travel was on foot, so they spent most of their lives in their village and the surrounding fields and woods.

FAMILY HOMES

Churls and their families lived in simple one-room homes. Their houses were built from planks of wood, with a thatched roof made from straw. At the centre of the family home was a fireplace with a metal cooking pot hanging over it. Most houses had no chimney and only slits for windows, so they were dark and smoky inside.

Anglo-Saxon family homes had very little furniture. People usually slept on simple wooden benches, which were also used as seats. The family's few possessions were kept in wooden chests or hung from pegs on the walls.

WORKING TOGETHER

Anglo-Saxon villagers often worked together. Groups of men went out hunting in teams, and brought back food for everyone to eat. Meat was usually roasted on an outdoor **spit** and everybody baked their bread in the large village oven. Women and girls gathered in the village weaving shed. Inside the shed, they span the village sheep's wool into thread and worked at large wooden looms, weaving blankets and clothes.

▲ The Anglo-Saxons cooked most of their meals in large metal cooking pots, which were hung over a fire.

▲ An image of feasting from the Bayeux tapestry. The table is covered with food and drink and a slave is serving the guests.

FAMILY MEALS

Most village families had simple meals of bread, vegetable stew and porridge. This basic diet was sometimes varied with eggs, milk and cheese from the village chickens, sheep and cows.

Village men and boys trapped birds and hares and caught fish to add to their family's diet. People of all ages washed down their food with watery ale.

VILLAGE FEASTS

The thane held regular feasts for all the villagers in his hall. People sat on benches at a long table and settled in for hours of eating and drinking.

The village feasts provided a chance for the churls and their families to eat a lot of meat. Usually, a pig was roasted on the village spit, and they also enjoyed wild deer and boar from the thane's forests.

PARENTS AND CHILDREN

Children were expected to help their parents as soon as they were old enough to work. This meant there was no room for a child who couldn't work and babies who were weak or disabled were usually left out in the cold to die. If a family was desperately poor, the parents sometimes made the tough decision to sell one or more of their children as slaves.

MARRYING YOUNG

Anglo-Saxon parents usually chose the person their child should marry. Some parents even signed a **marriage contract** for their son or daughter when the child was only seven years old. However, the marriage did not usually take place until the girl was 12 and the boy was 14.

▲ These two young children are dressed as an Anglo-Saxon girl and boy.

Sometimes a girl would be offered as a wife to a man from a rival tribe. By becoming the rival's wife, it was hoped that the girl would create peaceful links between the tribes. Girls who were offered in marriage to create a peace were known as 'peace-weavers'.

HONOURING THE DEAD

The Anglo-Saxons treated their **ancestors** with great respect. They held feasts in honour of dead warriors, and told stories and poems about their daring deeds.

When a great warrior died, he was given a solemn funeral. His body was dressed in armour and surrounded by weapons and treasures. In the early part of the Anglo-Saxon period people worshipped pagan gods and believed in an afterlife, in which warriors feasted in heavenly halls. The dead were buried with their possessions so that they could use them in the afterlife.

◄ These decorated shields were found in a warrior's grave at Sutton Hoo in Suffolk. You can find out more about the Sutton Hoo grave on page 21.

REAL LIVES

KENELM: A YOUNG PRINCE

Kenelm was the son of King Kenwulf of Mercia. When his father died in 819, the seven-year-old Kenelm inherited the Mercian throne, but he did not live to become king. An ancient legend tells that Kenelm was murdered by a jealous rival, and his body was hidden in a forest. Eventually, however, his body was found by monks, who buried the young prince with great honour beside his father. The story of Kenelm's death is probably mainly myth, but there was a real Prince Kenelm.

DID ANGLO-SAXON CHILDREN GO TO SCHOOL?

There were no schools in Anglo-Saxon England. Most adults and children could not read or write, but some monks and nuns were very well educated. Princes and princesses were taught by monks and nuns and learned to read and write Latin as well as English.

BEAUTIFUL BOOKS

For the few people who could read, there were beautiful books made by monks. Anglo-Saxon monks copied out Christian texts by hand and decorated their texts with patterns and pictures. These decorated books are known as illuminated manuscripts.

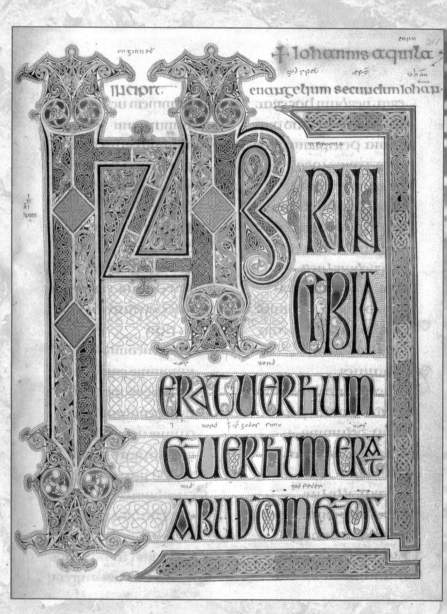

▲ This is a page from the Lindisfarne Gospels, a manuscript made by monks in northern England during the 8th century.

STORIES, POEMS AND RIDDLES

Anglo-Saxon children learned about their history and the world around them by listening to stories, songs and riddles. Long stories and poems combined history and legend in their tales of warriors, battles and adventures. Often, these stories were set to music and sung as songs.

Some Anglo-Saxon poems were written down, and are still read today. The most famous poem is *Beowulf*, which describes the adventures of a brave warrior lord, who fought battles and killed monsters to protect his people.

People told riddles to their children to help them think in new ways about familiar things. In one Anglo-Saxon riddle an object says "I do no harm to anyone unless they cut me first. Then I soon make them cry." Can you guess what the object is? (The answer is on page 29.)

REAL LIVES

BEDE: A MONK, A SCHOLAR AND A WRITER

Bede was born near Durham, in 673. At the age of seven, he was sent to Monkwearmouth Abbey, where he was taught by the abbot, Benedict Biscop. Bede studied Latin, Greek and Hebrew so he could read everything in the abbey library. When Bede grew up he became a monk. He spent the rest of his life at Monkwearmouth and its sister abbey in Jarrow. He was a great **scholar**, who wrote on a range of subjects, including religion, history, medicine, astronomy and science. Today, Bede's most famous book is **his** *Ecclesiastical History of the English People*.

WHAT JOBS DID ANGLO-SAXON PEOPLE DO?

Most people in Anglo-Saxon England had to work very hard just to stay alive. In the villages, people usually worked on the land, but some developed special craft skills. Men also trained to fight, and a few became traders.

▲ This illustrated calendar dates from about 1030. It shows farmers working together, ploughing a field and sowing seed.

FARMERS

Men, women and children worked in the fields around their village. Men led teams of oxen, pulling heavy wooden ploughs, while children scared away the birds. Older boys were often giving the job of herding cattle and sheep and keeping a lookout for wolves. Women and girls fed the village pigs and chickens, which were kept close to the houses.

Anglo-Saxon farmers grew wheat and rye for bread, barley for brewing beer, and oats for making porridge. They also grew a range of vegetables, including carrots, onions, cabbages and peas. Cows and sheep provided milk and cheese, and sheep's wool was woven into clothes and blankets. Pigs were the only animals kept for their meat.

CRAFTWORKERS

Within the villages, some people developed special skills. Woodworkers made chests, tables and benches and shaped wood into bowls. Leather workers made shoes, belts and bags, saddles and bridles for horses, and buckets for carrying water and milk. Potters made everyday dishes for cooking and eating. They also fashioned burial **urns** to hold the ashes of the dead.

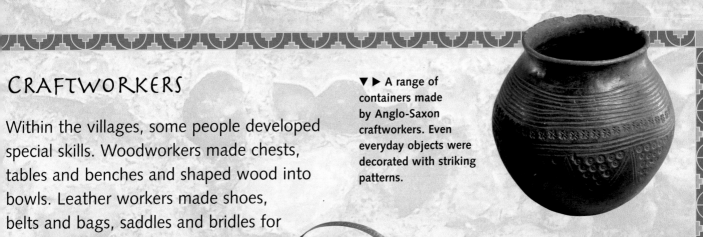

▼ ▶ A range of containers made by Anglo-Saxon craftworkers. Even everyday objects were decorated with striking patterns.

REAL LIVES

CAEDMON: A HERDSMAN AND A POET

The story of Caedmon is recorded by the monk, Bede (see page 17). According to Bede, Caedmon was a herdsman, who lived in the 7th century. His job was to look after the animals that belonged to Whitby Abbey in Yorkshire. He could not read or write, but he loved to hear the monks and nuns singing. One night Caedmon went to sleep with his animals, feeling sad because he knew no songs. But during the night he had a miraculous dream. In his dream, he heard a wonderful song and when he woke up he wrote it down. Caedmon the herdsman became a famous poet, composing and singing songs about God's creation.

▲ In July 2009 an amazing collection of gold and silver jewellery, plates, bowls and weapons was uncovered in a field in Staffordshire. The 'Staffordshire hoard' shows the remarkable skill of the Anglo-Saxon metalworkers.

METALWORKERS

Village smiths worked with iron to make useful items, such as horseshoes, tools, knives, and weapons. There were also some highly skilled metalworkers who worked with gold and silver and precious stones. These clever craftworkers were employed by kings and wealthy nobles to create fine jewellery, crowns, weapons and armour. They produced outstanding works of art, decorated with jewels and delicate engravings.

WARRIORS

Anglo-Saxon men did not have full-time jobs as soldiers, but all men trained for battle, so they were ready to fight whenever they were needed. Boys learned their fighting skills from their fathers and practised with their friends. Young churls learned to use a longbow and arrow, and practised fighting with spears and axes. Men from noble families taught their sons to ride on horseback and use a sword.

If an enemy attacked, thanes fought for their king, and churls fought for their thane. Anglo-Saxon soldiers wore metal helmets and carried large shields to protect themselves. Some of them wore suits of chainmail (hundreds of metal rings, linked tightly together).

TRADERS

Some Anglo-Saxon traders sailed north to Scandinavia. Others travelled to Russia, France and Italy and even reached the Middle East. Traders sailed in long, flat-bottomed boats, equipped with oars and a sail. They exchanged English wool and metalwork for jewels, furs and ornaments.

REAL LIVES

THE SUTTON HOO WARRIOR

In 1939, **archaeologists** discovered the remains of an Anglo-Saxon ship burial at Sutton Hoo, in Suffolk. The body had decayed, but there was plenty of evidence that the dead hero had been a great warrior. Inside the upturned warship were the remains of a decorated helmet (shown here) as well as a sword and shield, along with a purse, a golden buckle, and some bowls and drinking horns. Nobody knows exactly who the dead warrior was, but he was clearly a very important and wealthy man. He may have been King Raedwald, a successful **warlord** who ruled the East Angles from around 600 to 624.

WHAT DID ANGLO-SAXON ADULTS AND CHILDREN WEAR?

All the Anglo-Saxons wore the same simple styles, but materials for clothes varied according to class. In poor families, women and girls made all the family's clothes, using coarse wool that they spun and wove themselves. Rich people's clothes were made from fine wool or linen, and were often decorated with embroidery. Children wore smaller versions of their parents' clothes.

CLOTHES FOR MEN AND BOYS

Poor men and boys wore short tunics with a belt. When the weather was cold they added thick woollen cloaks and loose trousers, wrapped around their legs with thin strips of leather. Wealthy men and boys often wore long tunics and cloaks with embroidered borders.

CLOTHES FOR WOMEN AND GIRLS

Women and girls of all classes wore long dresses with belts. They usually covered their head with a scarf, and wore a cloak when the weather was cold.

Poor people's clothes were often left undyed, or coloured shades of yellow, brown or green, using natural dyes from plants. Rich people's clothes were coloured with more expensive natural dyes, such as scarlet and blue.

◄ Anglo-Saxon women and girls spent a lot of time making clothes. This group is from the living museum at West Stow village.

Jewellery and Charms

Men and women fastened their cloaks with a metal pin or brooch. Wealthy men and women wore elaborate brooches made from silver and gold, and **inlaid** with precious stones. Rich women wore beads and rings made from silver, gold, amber and ivory.

Men, women and children often wore an **amulet**, or lucky charm, around their necks. Amulets were stones or carvings which were believed to have magical powers. People believed that amulets could protect their wearers from disease and keep them safe in battle.

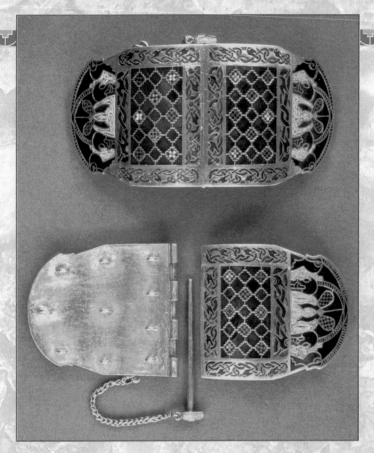

▲ This pair of decorated shoulder claps are made from gold and semi-precious stones. They were found in the warrior's grave at Sutton Hoo (see page 21).

REAL LIVES

A GLOUCESTERSHIRE PRINCESS

The grave of a very wealthy Anglo-Saxon woman has been found in Gloucestershire. The woman was clearly extremely rich because she was buried with over 500 treasures, including gold brooches, amber beads, and silver and ivory rings. Archaeologists think that the unknown woman must have been a local princess. They have nicknamed her "Mrs Getty" after the 20th-century millionaire J. P. Getty.

HOW DID ANGLO-SAXON ADULTS AND CHILDREN HAVE FUN?

All the Anglo-Saxons took time off from their work to enjoy themselves. In the countryside, there were holidays to mark special events in the farming year, such as sowing and harvesting, and kings and thanes held feasts in their halls.

OUTDOOR SPORTS

People gathered together on holidays to enjoy outdoor sports. Men and boys took part in competitions for running, jumping, swimming and wrestling. There were village ball games with large numbers of players, and tugs-of-war, when rival teams pulled as hard as they could on opposite ends of a rope, until one team collapsed in a heap.

Men from noble families enjoyed the sport of hunting, riding on horseback after deer or wild boar. They also practised their battle skills in mock sword fights. Churls held archery contests, using longbows and arrows.

▼ This 11th-century calendar shows a man enjoying the sport of falconry. Falcons were powerful hunting birds that were trained to catch smaller birds and bring them back to their masters.

INDOOR GAMES AND TOYS

People of all classes enjoyed indoor games. Men, women and children played a range of board games, using counters and dice. They also had an early form of chess. Children played a game of skill called 'knuckles', which involved picking up small stones in one hand as fast as they could.

Anglo-Saxon children had a range of simple toys. They played with carved wooden animals, ships and spinning tops. Girls had dolls made from cloth or wood and boys fought pretend battles with wooden swords. Children also had fun making music, using simple pipes made from reeds or animal bones.

FUN FEASTS

Anglo-Saxon feasts were a chance for everyone to relax and have fun. They lasted for many hours and people were entertained while they ate and drank. Musicians played on harps and pipes, and storytellers (known as *scops*) recited stories and poems, often accompanied by music.

Feasts varied greatly, from a small village event to a grand occasion hosted by a king. At special feasts, the guests were treated to a host of entertainers, including dancers, acrobats and jugglers.

▲ This is a modern copy of an Anglo-Saxon harp. Musicians played their harps at feasts and sang dramatic songs about great battles.

Jugglers were especially popular, and they sometimes added an element of danger to their act by juggling with knives instead of balls.

HOW IMPORTANT WAS RELIGION FOR THE ANGLO-SAXONS?

The Anglo-Saxon tribes who invaded England brought their religion with them. They worshipped gods and goddesses who had their origins in the Norse gods of the Viking people. Many Anglo-Saxons also believed in powerful nature spirits. They held outdoor ceremonies near springs and wells and close to special rocks and trees.

GODS AND GODDESSES

The early Anglo-Saxons had gods and goddesses for almost every aspect of their lives. They had a goddess of love, a god of war, and a god of metalworking. There was even a god of mischief, called Loki.

Some Anglo-Saxon gods gave their names to our days of the week. Tuesday was named after Tiw, the god of war. Wednesday gets its name from Woden, the ruler of the gods.

▲ Many Anglo-Saxon gods were based on Norse gods from Scandinavia. This tapestry shows (from left to right) the Norse gods Odin, Thor and Frey. The Anglo-Saxons called them Woden, Thor and Frigg.

Thursday belonged to Thor, the god of Thunder, and Friday was named after Frigg, the goddess of love.

CHRISTIANITY ARRIVES

In 597, the **Pope** sent a monk called Augustine to convert the English people to Christianity. Augustine preached to King Ethelbert of Kent and persuaded him to give up his old gods. Over the next few years, thousands of people in southern Britain became Christians, and Ethelbert made Augustine the first Archbishop of Canterbury.

REAL LIVES

CUTHBERT: SHEPHERD, SOLDIER, MONK AND BIRDLOVER

Cuthbert grew up in Scotland in the 7th century. As a young boy he worked as a shepherd, but at the age of 17 he decided to become a monk. After a few years, he left to fight as a soldier for his thane. Then, when he returned, he worked as a **missionary**, spreading the Christian message. At the age of 42, he moved to the Farne Islands, off the coast of Northumberland. Cuthbert was made Bishop of Lindisfarne, but he spent most of his time living alone in a cave. He is believed to have performed many miracles throughout his life. While he was on the Farne Islands, he introduced a law to protect the eider ducks that nested on the islands.

GLOSSARY

abbess A nun who is the head of an abbey or a convent.

amulet A charm that is believed to have magical powers, and is usually worn around the neck.

ancestors Family members who lived a long time ago.

archaeologist Someone who learns about the past by uncovering ancient buildings, graves and objects and examining them carefully.

ceremonies Special religious events or services.

churl A free man who swore loyalty to his lord (or thane). Churls and their families lived and worked on the thane's land and churls promised that they would fight for their thane in times of war.

convent A building in which nuns live and work.

convert To give up an old set of beliefs and join a new religion.

earl A powerful man who ruled a large area of the country.

earldom An area of a country that is ruled by an earl.

inlaid Set into another material.

longbow A very tall bow for shooting arrows.

marriage contract An agreement made between two families, promising that their children will marry sometime in the future.

missionary Someone who teaches people about a religion, such as Christianity.

myth An old story or legend, which may not be true.

pagan Not Christian.

Pope The head of the Roman Catholic Church.

reeds Plants with long hollow stems that grow near water.

scholar A very clever and learned person.

spit A horizontal rod that rests over a fire and has a joint of meat fixed to it. As the spit is turned, the meat roasts slowly on all sides.

thane A nobleman who owned land and usually lived in a large hall.

urns Pots that hold the ashes of dead people.

warlord A a man who leads his people into battle.

Witan A group of nobles who advised Anglo-Saxon kings about their country's laws.

Further Information

More books to read

Beowulf
Retold by Michael Morpurgo
and illustrated by Michael
Foreman
(Walker Books, 2007)

Moira Butterfiled
**Tracking Down:The Anglo-
Saxons in Britain**
(Franklin Watts, 2010)

Robert Hull
**British Heritage: The Anglo-
Saxons in Britain**
(Wayland, 2007)

Fiona Macdonald
**Anglo-Saxon and Viking
Britain**
(Franklin Watts, 2008)

Neil Tonge
**The History Detective
Investigates: The Anglo-
Saxons**
(Wayland, 2008)

Abigail Wheatley and Hazel
Maskell
Anglo-Saxons and Vikings
(Usborne, 2010)

Useful websites

www.bbc.co.uk/schools/primaryhistory/anglo
_saxons/
An interactive guide to Anglo-Saxon life, with
sections on growing up, stories and pastimes,
and Anglo-Saxon beliefs. Also includes an
archeology game called 'Dig it up'.

www.britishmuseum.org › Explore › Families
and children
Use the 'Museum Explorer' and click on Anglo-
Saxon England. Topics to explore include birds
and beasts, dress and ornament, gods and
spirits, leaders and rulers.

www.staffordshirehoard.org.uk/
A website on the hoard of Anglo-Saxon
treasures discovered in Staffordshire in
July 2009.

The answer to the riddle on page 17
is "an onion".

Places to visit

West Stow Anglo-Saxon village, Suffolk
A 'living museum' showing the village of
West Stow as it would have been in Anglo-
Saxon times.
http://www.stedmundsbury.gov.uk/weststow/

**The Sutton Hoo treasures in the British
Museum, London**
A collection of treasures discovered in the
Anglo-Saxon ship burial at Sutton Hoo.
http://www.britishmuseum.org/explore/young
_explorers/online_tours/sutton_hoo/sutton_ho
o.aspx

Bede's World, in Jarrow, Northumberland.
A museum presenting information on the life
and times of the Venerable Bede, who lived
from 673-735.

INDEX

Numbers in **bold** indicate pictures.